All About Romsey in the year 1607

> Master Samuel Adams
> the vicar of Romsey in 1607
> talks to the children of Romsey
> in the year 2007

Text: Barbara Burbridge

Illustrations: Rob Johnson

1607 - 2007

On the occasion of the
400th Anniversary
of
Romsey's
Royal Charter of Incorporation

A copy of this book
is to be presented by
Romsey Town Council
in March 2007
to every child attending
one of the following Romsey primary schools
**Cupernham Infant School
Cupernham Junior School
Halterworth Primary School
Romsey Abbey Primary School
Romsey Primary School**

A Romsey Town Council Publication
ISBN: 978 0 9555276 0 9
© Romsey Town Council (book)
© Rob Johnson (illustrations)

CONTENTS

Meet the Vicar of Romsey	5
King James I	7
Signing the Romsey Charter	9
Romsey and its Abbey Church	11
On the Way to the Market Place	13
The Market Place	17
Our Town Hall	19
Meeting the People	21
The Children of Romsey	23
Master Samuel Adams' House	25
What is a Borough?	28
What is a Parish?	29
What is a Royal Charter	30
Sealing a Royal Charter	31

Romsey's Mace
bought in 1672
In 2007 it is called 'the lesser mace' and is kept in the Town Hall.
drawn by Rob Johnson 2007

Master Samuel Adams, Vicar of Romsey 1590-1620
*An idea of how he may have looked
drawn by Rob Johnson 2007*

Meet the Vicar of Romsey

Good day to you. I hope this July weather is not too warm for you. We seem to have had nothing but hot dry days all summer.

By the way, my name is Master Samuel Adams, and I am the vicar of Romsey. So I am in charge of our beautiful Abbey church.

When I became the vicar seventeen years ago, the great Elizabeth Tudor was Queen of England. She was the daughter of the famous King Henry VIII. We often called her 'Good Queen Bess', and she was our queen for about 45 years. After such a long time, everyone felt lost when she died just four years ago in the year 1603.

Now we have a new king.

The Stuart Kings & Queens of England

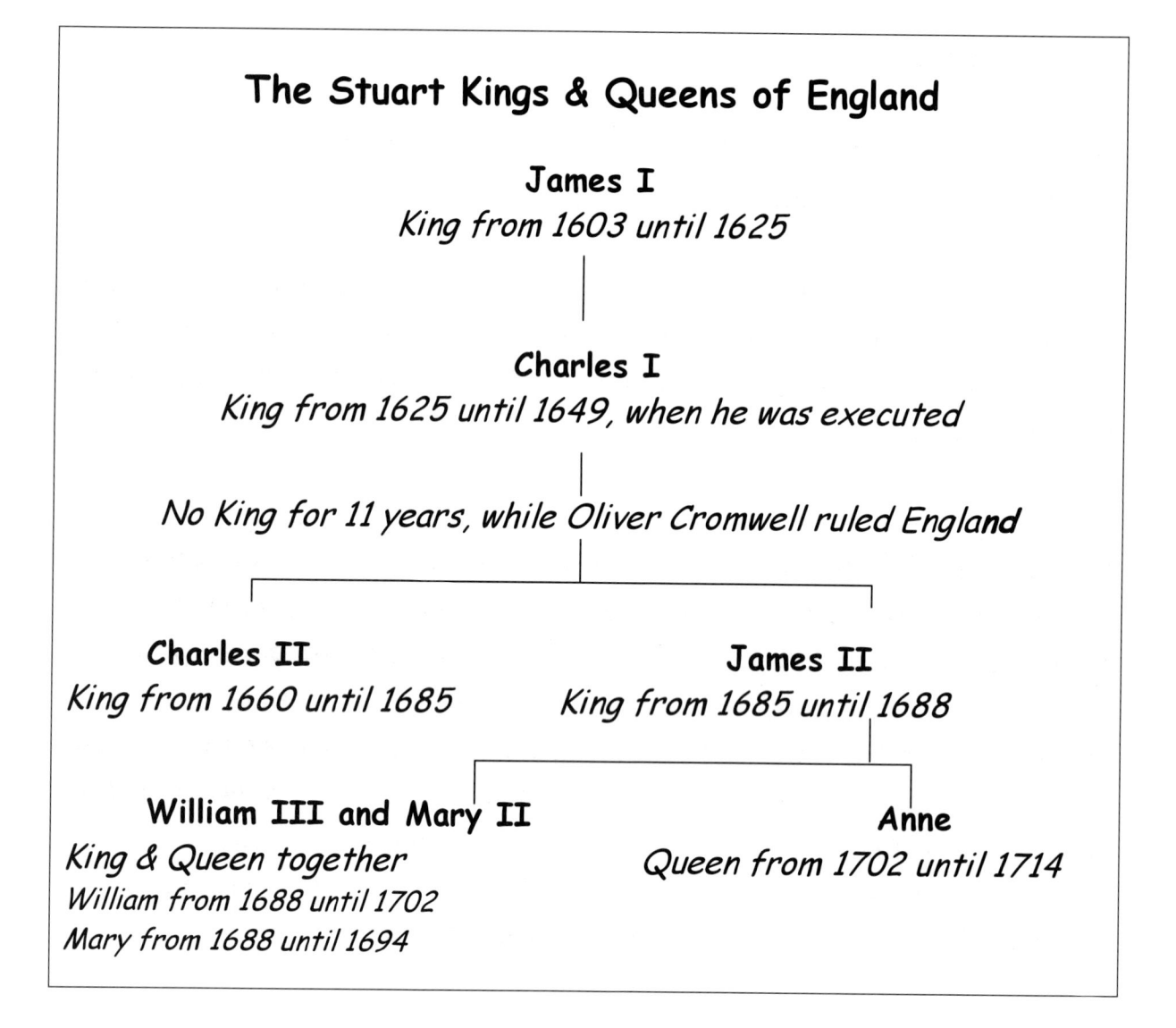

James I
King from 1603 until 1625

Charles I
King from 1625 until 1649, when he was executed

No King for 11 years, while Oliver Cromwell ruled England

Charles II
King from 1660 until 1685

James II
King from 1685 until 1688

William III and Mary II
King & Queen together
William from 1688 until 1702
Mary from 1688 until 1694

Anne
Queen from 1702 until 1714

Can you make your own family tree?

King James I

Our new king is called James Stuart, and he was Queen Elizabeth's cousin. He had to come down to England from Scotland.

He is the first king called James that we have had in England. Perhaps there will be many more with that name just as we have already had eight kings called Henry. In that case he will be called King James I.

Poor King James had a worrying time about two years ago. A group of men who did not want him to be king decided that they would try to kill him. They planned to blow up the Houses of Parliament when he was paying a visit there. We call their plan the Gunpowder Plot.

One of the plotters was a man by the name of Guy Fawkes but he was caught before anything nasty could happen. Now we remember the great day when the King was saved - 5th November 1605. Some people are beginning to call it Bonfire Night, because we have bonfires to celebrate the day the King was saved.

The Great Seal of James I
A seal like this hangs at the bottom of Romsey's 1607 Charter
drawn by Rob Johnson 2007

Signing the Romsey Charter

Just this year, on 6th April and far away at Westminster in London, King James signed and sealed a royal charter making our little town of Romsey into a borough. We all feel very proud to live in such an important place.

Now we hear that King James himself is coming for a short visit next month at the beginning of August. We're not sure whether we'll see much of him. He's bound to spend most of his time at Broadlands House on the edge of town.

That's the home now of the St Barbe family, but some of the very old people can just remember that it used to be the farmlands of the nuns of Romsey Abbey. That was before 1539, when King Henry VIII was closing down all the monasteries and nunneries in the land. All the Romsey nuns were sent away and their lands and buildings sold to private buyers.

There are some special pages at the end of this book to tell you the meanings of words like **charter** and **borough**.

Romsey Abbey
There was no bell tower or clock in 1607
drawn by Rob Johnson 2007

Romsey and its Abbey Church

Well, I've told you about our exciting year so far, and how proud we are to have become a borough.

Now I'd like to take you around the town. I think we should start by looking at our lovely old church.

Not many towns have such a large and grand building to be its parish church. The reason we have such a big church is that it was built for those nuns who used to be here in Romsey. They were quite rich.

On the south side of the Abbey church, the nuns had the buildings where they lived. It was private with a great wall all around. The townspeople and their vicar of those days only had a small part of the church on the north side. It was so small that they had to knock through the north wall and build an extension.

It is now nearly 70 years since King Henry VIII sent all the nuns away. A few years after that had happened, in 1544, King Henry sold the whole of the church to us, and that is why we have such a great big building. We paid the King £100 for our church. What a lot of money that was.

Once we had the whole church for the town we no longer needed the extension. So we pulled it down. But there's not much money left for repairs, and I'm afraid we've had to mend the old wall in a rather patchy way.

Romsey Abbey north side
A modern photograph that shows the patchy wall. Perhaps you can go and look at it yourselves in 2007.

But come inside. The stones here are painted white or covered in writings now in 1607, but they used to be bright with wall paintings. They told some of the stories from the Bible and about the lives of especially good people called saints. And there was another painting of saints on a great wooden board. The last Abbess, Elizabeth Ryprose, had that done. But we were ordered to paint over all these pictures with plain whitewash, and then add on prayers and other words for people to recite in church. Some of the older folk still miss the colourful picture stories.

On the Way to the Market Place

Let's go out by the north door of the Abbey. Can you see our belfry tower over there to the right of the graveyard? That's where the parish bells are hung. Now that we have the whole church building, we are trying to save up money to have some new bells to hang in the main tower, but it's taking a long time to collect enough money. When we have the bells inside the Abbey church we can pull down the old belfry tower.

The parish bell tower
*How it may have looked
drawn by Rob Johnson 2007*

If we turn right out of the north door, we can walk across to Church Street. We have to cross a bridge over a stream to get there. I wonder if the water will be covered in one day.

I'm afraid all the waterways in town are smelly. That's because all the houses and workshops let their rubbish go out into the water.

The house of Anthony Petty, dyer of woollen cloth
His son, William, became famous in London.
This house stood in Church Street until it was destroyed by fire in the 1820s. Fortunately, a Romsey man called Dr John Latham drew the house just a few years before the fire.
drawn by Rob Johnson 2007

It's very busy here in Church Street. The people who live along here are tradesmen, making and then selling the things they make in their workshops.

There's a tall building along to the left on the way north. That's the home of the Petty family. They are dyers of woollen cloth.

The house that belonged to the Brackley family
(No 25 Church Street)
Perhaps it looked like this in 1607
drawn by Rob Johnson 2007

And across the road is a house that the Brackley family own. They have made their money from the woollen cloth trade, too.

Mind you, there aren't many very old houses in the town. Most of them are made of timber and that rots after a while. But the Petty house is an old house that has lasted because the bottom part is built of brick and stone. We're beginning to build more strong houses these days.

And there's one very old house in this street that was built completely of stone. It's straight ahead of us as we walk from the Abbey. It is unusual to find a stone house in Romsey because stone has to come from a long way away. Our stone house is very strong, and if you go and have a look you'll seen that they've just added on an extension made of timbers filled in with wattle and daub. There's a brazier living and working there. He makes things from bronze - pots, pans and, sometimes, small bells.

If we turn right we can walk down to the Market Place. You'll be able to see an important inn on the corner. It's called The Swan. Perhaps you can still see a sign with the picture of a swan on it today. That's our Swan Inn.

I wonder if any of these buildings I've shown you will last for hundreds of years for people of the future to see.

The Market Place

The great market place is at the middle of our town. It's just outside the main gateway into the old Abbey courtyard. That made it easy for the Abbess to collect the money that market traders had to pay her to have a stall in the Market Place. Now they all have to pay the mayor because the charter has made him Clerk of the Market.

There are three main streets off the Market Place. Church Street, where we've just been, goes off to the north and there's Mill Street going south over there. They are both very old streets.

The third way goes east towards Winchester. There's a new road there, which we are beginning to call The Hundred, but it's not part of the borough of Romsey.

Let me explain.

At the far end from the Abbey gateway the Market Place gets narrower. This is because we have a bridge where The Hundred now begins. On the other side of the bridge is Romsey Extra. Extra is a word that means outside, and Romsey Extra is outside the bridge.

Infra means inside, and Romsey Infra is inside the bridge. Only Romsey Infra is the important borough.

If we go down to that end of the Market Place, we'll pass another great inn. This one is called the White Horse. It's built with huge timbers and is very grand. Let's go just past there and have a look at Romsey's town hall.

Romsey's First Town Hall
(now No 23 Market Place)
drawn by Rob Johnson 2007

Our Town Hall

Now that we have become a borough, we all want to show how important we are. So the new corporation is renting a building as our very first town hall.

Everyone decided that the best place would be this house just by the bridge. It belongs to Robert Brackley, who owns another house round in Church Street. He is one of the men named in the charter as a member of the new Corporation. He is a chief burgess.

The idea is that the upstairs will be a meeting place for the mayor, six aldermen and twelve chief burgesses who are the members of the corporation. They will be able to make all the rules for the town there.

The town constable will have a room downstairs on the left, and there will be cells alongside where he can lock up wrongdoers. The cells are to be next to the stream so they may be a bit damp.

Anyway, the constable will be able to see everyone coming into and out of our new borough across the bridge. Wrongdoers had better take care.

The Swan Inn in the Market Place
*This inn was on the corner of the Market Place
and Church Street*
On Saturdays the great space of the Market Place would be filled with tradesmen's stalls and hurdle pens for cows, sheep and pigs. People came from far and wide to buy things at the weekly market.
drawn by Rob Johnson 2007

Meeting the People

While we are by the town hall, I suggest we walk around the Market Place and look at all the people out and about the town.

Romsey has never been one of the big towns but it is beginning to grow. There must be about 2,000 people living here now. All the same, most people know one another at least by sight, so today many are meeting a friend and stopping to chat.

Here's John Bloyse, our mayor, named in the charter. I expect he's been in the town hall. Look, he has stopped to speak to young Clare Syms. She likes to wave her hands around when she's talking. Then everyone can see the gold rings that her grandmother left for her when she died a few years ago.

And over the far side of the Market Place I can see John Hayward. He has plenty of money and he doesn't have to work. So we call him a gentleman. He's one of the important people and has been chosen as one of the six men named as aldermen in our new charter. He's a close friend of another alderman - Thomas Brackley the clothier. We all think they would like John's daughter, Christian, to marry Robert Brackley.

Just at the moment, though, it looks as if John is on his way to see Mr Gasse the butcher, another member of the Corporation. The Gasse family have been butchers for as long as anyone can remember. Sometimes they do get into trouble when they leave their butcher's block outside in the Pigmarket. And they get into trouble for selling meat when they shouldn't.

We'd better walk quickly now, or someone will be stopping us and I could be gossiping all day.

Boys playing in the Market Place
from a drawing by Rob Johnson 2007

The Children of Romsey

Have you noticed how many children there are in Romsey? It's the same wherever you go. There are nearly as many children under 16 years old as there are grown-ups. That's because there aren't many really old people.

Things are getting a little better now but a lot of people die every year and only the lucky ones live to be over 50 years old. Babies and small children often die, too, but enough live to fill the streets and help their fathers and mothers with their work.

Not many Romsey children go to school. You have to belong to families who can afford to send you to school. Some lucky ones learn to read and write a little if their parents can teach them. And when they are older some learn to read by studying the prayers and other religious words that are painted in such large letters on our Abbey walls. But most boys and girls just learn about work by watching the grown-ups.

From an early age, children have to be helpful. Farmers' sons start by scaring off the birds from the crops in the fields or picking up stones in the way of the plough.

Tradesmen's sons have to sweep the workshop floors, fetch and carry, and run messages.

The girls help their mother with the housework and getting food ready. They have to learn to make cheese and bake bread. Their hands soon get worn from scrubbing dirty clothes and lighting the fire. Often they have to look after younger brothers and sisters.

So children are very busy but they still have time to play. Did you notice the two boys kicking a ball near the town hall? They sometimes get up to mischief, trying out workmen's tools when they're not looking. Then they like to go and sail nutshells in the streams. Or they may play knucklebones - a game that you may call dibs or jacks.

Some girls like to copy their brothers if they can, but they also enjoy dancing and singing, or sewing.

Master Samuel Adams' House

Would you like to end our Romsey walk by coming into my house?

We have four main rooms – a hall, our best room called the parlour, the chamber over the parlour and an inner chamber. Then there's the kitchen, and a couple of stores called the buttery and little buttery. Outside there's a mill house where we can grind corn to make our own flour, a meal house for sifting the flour, an apple loft, a barn and stables.

Milling by Hand

There was a milling house behind Samuel Adams' home. Perhaps a servant ground the corn into flour for the family.
drawn by Rob Johnson 2007

I keep two mares for riding around the parish, and a colt. We also have a cow and a few pigs, together with hens and geese in a field nearby. Anyone with enough space tries to keep some animals, even in the town.

But let's go indoors. Even though it has been so hot and dry this summer, we have to keep a fire alight in the hall all the time because this is where we do much of the cooking. So we need those bellows to blow air into the fire to keep it going. What do you think of our huge fireplace with two spits for roasting meat and lots of cooking pots that we hang over the fire.

The parlour is cooler on a day like today, and I think it's even better than the hall anyway. We have so many more luxury items than most people - a cupboard for keeping glassware in, cushions, painted cloths hanging around the room, a looking-glass and bowls made of silver and gilt. My favourite thing here is my chessboard. And then I also have my private study of books. Only a few people can read well, and even they do not often have their own books.

And here is my dear wife, Margery, waiting to offer you something to eat and drink - something to cool you before going out into the hot sun again.

I am lucky to have such a comfortable home. Some of my poorest parishioners have nothing, and have to be looked after by the church's Overseers of the Poor.

And now I must get ready to go back to the church. It's the fifteenth day of July, so Richard Fachen is bringing his new baby daughter to be baptised this afternoon. I think she's going to be called Margaret. There's always work for a vicar to do.

I bid you farewell. I hope you have enjoyed your time with me here in Romsey in this special year of 1607.

Perhaps you can write or draw about Romsey in 1607 and how different it is today. What things do you have that you think would amaze the people of 1607?

What is a Borough?

A borough town is a town that has been made a bit more important than an ordinary one.

It has been given royal permission to have a corporation - a sort of council - to look after the town. We can now have a mayor as the chief citizen with some other people specially chosen to belong to the corporation. They are called aldermen and chief burgesses. They have a town clerk to do office work for them.

A borough town can make its own local laws. It may also have permission to hold its own local court of law. Romsey has got its own court now with a lawyer called the Court Recorder in charge of it. He has two sergeants-at-mace to help him.

Usually, a borough also has the right to hold fairs and markets. Our mayor has been made clerk of Romsey market.

We have been given a High Steward to watch over everyone. We feel very proud that the very first one is none other than the Earl of Southampton.

What is a Parish?

A parish is a district or area of land with its own church. All the people who live in that parish are called the parishioners.

In the year 1607, it is the law of the land that all parishioners over the age of 16 years must go to their church service every Sunday. If they do not go they have to pay a fine.

The vicar is the priest who takes the church service. He and his helpers look after the poor and those in need. He also keeps a great book called a register in which he writes down the names of all those who have been buried or baptised or married in his parish church.

What is a Royal Charter?

A royal charter is a very important piece of writing. It is signed and sealed by the King of England.

Lots of people make ordinary charters. These are the papers that they sign when they want to do something like sell a house, but they are not as special as a royal charter.

Our royal charter is called a charter of incorporation. This is because it 'incorporates' or makes Romsey into a borough.

I've seen the Romsey charter, and very important it looks, too. At the very beginning there's a picture of the king sitting in all his glory, and the first words are written in huge letters. And you should see the size of the royal seal at the end of the document. It is a great circle of wax and the king has pressed his own seal stamp onto it.

King James signed and sealed our charter at Westminster on Monday, 6th April 1607.

Sealing a Royal Charter

When the king signs a special document like the one for Romsey, his own great seal is added. This proves that it really is a royal grant and not just a pretend one that someone else has made. The seal is carefully guarded so no one can use it without the king's permission.

When the writing on a document is finished then a lump of hot wax is added. While the wax is still hot and soft the king's great seal is pressed into it to make a picture in the wax.

Each new monarch has his or her own seal designed and made.

Perhaps you could draw a seal for yourself or your school.

The production costs of this book have been shared by
Hampshire County Council
&
Romsey Town Council

Acknowledgements

Romsey Town Council wishes to thank Hampshire County Council for the support received, and Barbara Burbridge and Rob Johnson for having written and illustrated this book without charge.

Information for the book has come mainly from the records and research of local historians of the LTVAS Group (Lower Test Valley Archaeological Study Group). They are always pleased to help anyone who wants to find out more about the history of Romsey.